Comments for Report Cards and Notes Home

by
Audrey Clifford Lang

Table of Contents

Welcome Back Messages

Summer vacation is rushing by and your new students are becoming excited about the first day of school. Hearing from you can help ease students' fears and make the transition back to school easier.

Hello, my name is _____, and I will be your _____ grade teacher this fall. Our class will meet in room _____. It is located _____. There will be _____ (number) other students in our class. I know we will all have a great year together. See you on _____ (date)!

I hope you are enjoying your vacation. I wanted to tell you a little about what we will be doing this year. I am planning many fun and exciting activities at school, including field trips, assemblies, projects, and experiments. I love to read and will be sharing some of my favorite books with you. If you have a favorite book that you would like to share with the class, please let me know when school begins.

Congratulations! You're going to be in the _____ grade! Some of the things we will be learning about are _____. I look forward to having you in my class.

The start of the new school year is almost upon us. I am really looking forward to meeting you. When you come to school, go to room _____. Please bring the following items with you to start the year: a pencil, a notebook and paper, one of your favorite books, something you would like to share with your classmates about your summer vacation, and one question you would like to find the answer to this school year. (You may adjust list to fit your needs.)

Welcome to the _____ grade! My name is _____, and I will be your new teacher. This will be my first year at _____ (name of your school), and I am very excited about the upcoming year. We will be exploring new topics and learning many new things. I am really looking forward to meeting you.

Comments for the Beginning of the School Year

The beginning of the school year can be an exciting and traumatic time for both students and parents. There will be a new schedule, a new teacher, and many new expectations. It is an important time to get to know students and share information with the students' parents/guardians.

Adjusting Well

You should be very proud of _____. She is a well-adjusted _____ grade student! This has been a busy month, with everyone getting to know each other and adjusting to new schedules. She has been doing very well and seems to be comfortable and happy in class.

It is hard to believe that we have already been back in school for a month! I just wanted you to know that _____ has adjusted well to the _____ grade. He has adapted to the routine and actively participates in class. He seems eager to share his ideas and puts forth a lot of effort in class.

I am really enjoying getting to know _____. She is a very good student, and I can always count on her to lend a helping hand to her classmates. We are all pleased to have _____ as part of our class.

_____ is off to a wonderful start. We have been reviewing last year's material, and he has a good grasp of the concepts. He comes to school prepared and ready to work and is eager to get into the day's activities.

_____ is a pleasure to have in class. She has settled into her new schedule and has adjusted quite nicely to the new surroundings and routine. She is attentive and courteous in class and is putting forth an earnest effort.

It is a delight to have _____ in class. Although he tends to be on the quiet side, he does not hesitate to try new things. He is eager to participate, takes suggestions well, and puts forth an excellent effort. I am very pleased with how well he has adjusted to the new school year.

Difficulty Adjusting

_____ seems to be having some problems making friends this year. It may be helpful to suggest he invite a friend or friends for a special outing or visit. Perhaps you could also encourage him to participate in an after-school activity he would enjoy.

The school year began well, and _____ seemed to be adjusting well and making new friends. Recently, however, he has been having some behavior problems in class. I am a little concerned and think we should talk before this becomes a serious problem.

_____ is having a difficult time sitting quietly and is disrupting her neighbors. It seems to be hard for her to pay attention, and this is resulting in some academic problems. I would like to schedule a conference with you to discuss how we can help _____ overcome this problem before it becomes a major issue.

_____ seems to be having a few problems settling in this year. I have noticed that he is very quiet around his classmates and is often hesitant to join in group activities. I believe there are some things we can do to help _____ feel more comfortable. I will call you to discuss the situation.

_____ seldom joins in with her classmates and seems to prefer to be alone. I am encouraging her to work and play with a few students with whom she seems most comfortable and expect the situation will improve with time.

As the first few weeks of the school year have passed, I have noticed that _____ seems to have a tendency to be aggressive toward his peers. When things do not appear to be going his way, he can become bossy or angry. Perhaps we should talk before this becomes a serious problem.

_____ seems to be having a difficult time dealing with her anger and often directs it at her classmates. I will call you to arrange a time for us to meet and discuss this situation.

During these first couple of weeks of school, _____ has been experiencing some separation issues. He is very sad in the morning and does not want to come into class and start the day. I had hoped that it would lessen after the first couple of weeks but that has not been the case. Once he gets caught up in the day's activities, he seems to be okay. I would like for us to discuss this and see if we can think of some ways to help _____ feel more comfortable.

Difficulty Adjusting (continued)

School has been in session for a few weeks, and I am becoming concerned that _____ seems to be having difficulty getting organized. She forgets to bring her materials to school and often cannot find her pencil (or notebook, homework, or other item). Perhaps a book bag, backpack, or tote bag would help _____ keep her school things together.

Although it is early in the year, it is apparent that _____ is having some trouble with _____ (subject). Since extra help and support may be needed in this area, I would like to have _____ (a tutor, the resource teacher, a volunteer, etc.) work with him a few times a week.

_____ is adjusting nicely to school and seems to be making new friends. I have noticed, however, that she is having a difficult time with _____ (subject area). I would like to schedule a conference with you to discuss her progress and to develop a plan to help her. I am available most afternoons from _____ until _____. Please let me know what day and time would be convenient for you. I look forward to talking with you.

Language Arts

Reading, writing and general language arts skills are key components to a student's success. Now is the time when the building blocks of a child's future success will be laid. Parents need to understand on what level their child is functioning. If they are willing to be active participants in their child's education, then they need to know how they can help their child succeed.

Reading

I am very pleased to tell you that _____ knows all of the sounds of the alphabet and is very good at sounding out words. These skills will help him become a strong reader.

I am very pleased with _____'s progress. He easily recognizes all basic sight words and can use them in sentences.

_____ is a fluent reader. She enjoys reading on her own and participating in book discussions.

_____ is finding it challenging to learn all the sounds of the alphabet. I will be sending home some suggested activities you might do together to help him. Once he has mastered these sounds, I believe he will be ready to start reading our beginning readers independently.

_____ is having difficulty sounding out unfamiliar words. I think it would help her if you and she spent a few minutes each evening sounding out words in her textbooks and library books.

_____ does not immediately recognize all the basic sight words but is working hard to learn them. _____ has made a personal set of sight word flash cards to work with every day. He will be bringing them home. Please work with him on these a few times a week.

_____ needs to work on developing better comprehension skills. I will be sending home short readings with comprehension questions several times a week. It would help to speed up _____'s improvement if you would review _____'s work before she brings it back to school.

I feel that _____ would really benefit from reading more outside of school. Call me if you would like some suggestions for how to help him to enjoy reading more.

Reading (continued)

I am a little concerned because _____ does not seem to retain enough of what he reads. Many times he has to reread a story or passage before answering comprehension questions. I believe that the more he reads the better his comprehension skills will become. It would be very helpful if you could encourage _____ to read for twenty minutes every night and then take five or ten minutes to tell you about what he has read.

At this time, _____ reads at a slow pace and does not seem to enjoy reading. I plan to send home materials that I feel will interest her. It is my hope that _____'s reading speed and enjoyment will increase the more she reads.

I am pleased that _____ loves books and reading. Although it may be just a matter of time before he is reading on grade level, right now he is struggling. Please encourage him to keep reading as much as possible and to make sure he does not become frustrated trying to read books that are too difficult. When you read at home it may be helpful not to let _____ struggle too long with a word before offering help. As he gains confidence and his ability improves we can gradually back away from helping.

_____ is still struggling with reading and comprehension. When you are reading together and she stumbles on a word, she should just spell it and continue reading until the end of the sentence. She may figure out the word through context clues. If not, at least her thinking will not have been interrupted until the end of the sentence. This may help her comprehension.

_____ needs to work on developing better critical thinking and deductive reasoning skills. He has a particularly hard time predicting what will happen next or what the outcome will be. I will be sending home some short readings and accompanying questions designed to help _____ develop his critical thinking and deductive reason skills.

Writing

_____'s written work and overall effort have been quite good this past grading period. He took his assignments seriously and worked conscientiously. His last writing piece was excellent.

_____ enjoys writing and has a wonderful command of her spelling and vocabulary words.

_____ has excellent sequencing skills which carry over to his writing skills. He clearly understands that every paragraph or story must have a beginning, a middle, and an end and writes accordingly. I want you to know how pleased I am with his progress.

I am very happy to see that _____ has no problem writing in complete sentences. She is having a hard time, however, writing paragraphs. We will be doing more activities in class that I believe will help her develop better paragraph writing skills.

_____ loves to write short stories, but he has a difficult time making sure they have a beginning, a middle, and an end (or other skill). We will be working on this in class with a combination of writing and sequencing activities that I believe will help.

_____ does not seem to be enjoying our writer's workshop. She is having a difficult time putting her wonderful story ideas into words. It might help if you would encourage her to tell stories at home.

_____ is having a hard time putting his thoughts on paper. I will be encouraging him to do extra journal writing activities in order to help him in class. You may want to get _____ a journal (or diary) and encourage him to write in it three or four times a week at home.

_____ needs to develop better descriptive writing skills. Although _____ really enjoys writing, she has a difficult time including descriptive words and uses very few adjectives or adverbs. I will be encouraging _____ to reread her stories and to go back and add descriptive words. Perhaps when reading together at home you could discuss how the author describes a character or scene.

_____ is having some difficulties writing in complete sentences. I will be sending home a series of worksheets over the next few weeks designed to help him develop a better understanding of how to form sentences. It would be helpful if you would review each assignment.

Writing (continued)

_____ needs some help with her book reports. I believe it would be very helpful if you would talk with _____ about each book she reads. Let her tell you the story and talk about her favorite parts before she starts writing her book report. I think this will help her better organize her thoughts.

We have been working on letter writing activities this week. While we will be moving on to another topic next week, _____ still needs more practice. It would be helpful if you could give him the names and addresses of three or four people to whom he could write a letter with your guidance.

_____ needs to work on the writing process we use. She does not like to write a first draft, revise the first draft, correct it, have her writing partner edit it, and then write a final copy. _____ seems to feel the process takes too much time. We have discussed her feelings, and I have explained that I expect her to write at least one story a week using this process.

_____ needs to do a better job proofreading her writing. I would suggest that you have her show you her writing assignments before she brings them to school.

_____ is having a difficult time with verb tenses (or other skill) when writing a story. He is working on making a "verb book," which will list verbs by past, present, and future tenses (or other strategy for learning the skill). I believe this will help him gain a better understanding of verb tenses and how to use them.

_____ enjoys writing but is having trouble with the rules for punctuation and capitalization. We will be working on these skills in class, but I think he would benefit from doing a workbook at home. If you cannot find a workbook on punctuation and capitalization, I will be happy to send home some supplemental worksheets.

_____ often uses punctuation marks incorrectly. I believe this is due more to carelessness and not thinking about which marks to use than not understanding how to use them. I will be sending home punctuation activities for her to do until I see an improvement in her class work.

Oral Communication Skills

_____ has a difficult time expressing himself verbally. It might help if during the evening you could encourage him to talk about his day and how he feels about school.

_____ is a very good reader, but she needs to practice reading aloud with fluency and expression. Please encourage her to practice reading aloud to you at home. It would also be helpful for you to read aloud to her.

_____ is having a difficult time talking in front of a group or giving an oral presentation. We are going to be working on developing public speaking skills in class over the next few months. It might be helpful if you could let him practice reading out loud in front of you or the family.

I am a concerned that _____ does not pronounce some words clearly. I will be calling you to discuss my concerns and set up a meeting. I am sure that together we can come up with a plan to help her work on her pronunciation.

Spelling

_____ is doing very well on her weekly spelling words and spelling assignments. Please encourage her to keep up the good work.

_____ has a great imagination and loves writing stories but needs to work on his spelling and grammar skills. I have given him a set of activity sheets to work on both in school and at home, which I believe will help him in these areas. It might help if you work with _____ on some of these activity sheets a couple of times a week.

_____ would benefit from spending more time reviewing her spelling words. A quick review each evening may be all that is required to see an improvement.

_____ is having some difficulty with spelling. _____ will be making her own personal dictionary for her most frequently misspelled words. Please take a few minutes two or three times a week and quiz _____ on the words in her dictionary.

Spelling (continued)

_____ needs to spend time studying the rules on how to make words plural (or other skill). We will be reviewing the rules in class, and I will be sending home a list of words and their plurals. Perhaps you could spend five or ten minutes each evening asking _____ to spell the plurals of a few of the words on the list.

Penmanship

_____ has wonderful penmanship for her age. It is a delight to read her work. Tell her to keep up the good work!

_____ needs to spend more time practicing his penmanship. It might help if he practiced at home ten minutes a night three times a week, just copying a favorite storybook or an article from the newspaper if he cannot think of anything to write.

Penmanship seems to be a real challenge for _____. She is working on tracing letters in class and will be doing some homework that should improve her skills.

Other

_____ loves reading, writing, and sharing her ideas. Her overall effort and participation have been excellent.

_____ is having a difficult time recognizing parts of speech (or other skill). I will be sending home some extra worksheets for her to do over the next few weeks, which should help.

Dictionary and alphabetizing skills do not seem to come easily to _____. I believe he just needs more practice and his skills will improve. I will be giving him some extra activities to help him. Perhaps you could work with him and look up two or three words in the dictionary each night or make up a list of five or six random words to be put in alphabetical order.

_____ is struggling to expand his vocabulary and use a broader variety of words in his everyday writing. I will be giving him a word a day to use in his writing and speech. Perhaps you could help _____ set up a word box at home where he could keep his special words.

Math

Whether your students become business executives, cashiers, chefs, homemakers, teachers, or lawyers, they will need to have mastered basic math skills in order to succeed. Getting parents to be active participants in their children's learning is vital to the students' success.

Succeeding or Improving

_____ is progressing nicely in math and is working on grade level.

_____ is an outstanding student in math. She grasps all of the concepts and seems to easily learn the facts.

Math is _____'s best subject. He is doing well and working on grade level.

_____'s success in math this year has been a very positive experience for her and has really helped build her self-confidence.

_____ has shown great improvement in math but needs to continue the extra work she has been doing with you at home each night in order stay on track.

I am very pleased with _____'s progress. Using manipulatives has already helped him gain a better understanding of place value (or other skill).

_____ is doing well in math this quarter. Please encourage him to continue to work hard.

_____ has made excellent progress and should be proud of how far she has come in math this year.

_____ should be very proud of himself. He has made a conscious effort to improve his math skills. Although progress has been slow, he has not given up. We need to continue to provide all of the encouragement we can, both here at school and at home.

_____ has improved dramatically in math. I think this was the result of our joint efforts and I want to thank you for the help and support you provided at home.

Succeeding or Improving (continued)

_____ understands basic concepts of numbers and sets (or other skill). She is ready to move on to more advanced math skills. We will be working on _____ next.

_____ can tell time and work with money. He now needs to spend time working on basic addition and subtraction skills.

Although _____ is still having difficulty with division (or other skill), she is making progress. There is still a lot of work to be done, however, if she is going to master this and move on to more difficult skills. Please continue to review her work at home.

Needs Practice

_____ has a hard time grasping new math concepts. It would be helpful if you could encourage him to discuss the day's math activities at home. I think that having him explain and review the day's concepts with you will help him gain a better understanding.

_____'s work has been inconsistent in class. She needs help understanding the basic concepts of addition (or other skill). We can discuss this on the phone or set up a conference to review what we can do to help _____ get back on track.

Word problems (or other skill) continue to be a challenge for _____. I think that if we had a conference we could plan a strategy that would help _____ develop a better grasp of this skill.

_____ is struggling a little with math. He is having a hard time applying the concepts he has learned to solve the problems we are doing. I believe he just needs some extra practice. I am sending home some extra work with him that I think will help. Please review this work with him each night.

_____ could benefit from spending more time using manipulatives in class. She is having a hard time with the concept of place value (or other skill), and I believe she will have more success with the visual examples manipulatives can offer.

Needs Practice (continued)

_____ needs more help developing his problem solving and deductive reasoning skills. He is having a difficult time with these higher-level skills. I will be sending home some activities that should help.

_____'s strength seems to be memorizing the basic math facts. In order to help her become more successful in higher-level math skills, you may want to encourage her to do some fun logic and word problems books, available in the children's section at most book stores.

_____ appears to have a difficult time with the concept of fractions (or other skill). I would suggest that we have a phone conference and that I send extra work home at least twice a week for you and him to do together. Perhaps you could point out to him some everyday examples of fractions. For instance, the next time you have pizza at home you could talk about how the whole is cut into fractions (or other activity).

_____ needs to spend more time at night reviewing what we have done in class. She is having a very hard time with the concept of place value (or other skill). I believe, however, that if she will put in some extra review time she will grasp the concept fairly quickly.

Estimation is a hard skill, and _____ is having a difficult time with it. If you could work with him at home and make it a game, it would be very helpful. For example, if you are having a roasted chicken for dinner, ask _____ how much he thinks the chicken weighs. Ask him to guess how long a rug is, how tall you are, how tall his brothers and sisters are, how much water is in a glass, etc., and then measure to check his estimates. The more he tries to estimate the better he will become at it.

Equivalent fractions (or other skill) are presenting _____ with her hardest math challenge this year. I will be sending extra work home with her, and it would really help _____ if you would assist her with it.

Factoring (or other skill) seems to be a challenge for _____. Although he is having a hard time with it now, I think with a little practice he will master it without any problem.

_____ does a great job subtracting single-digit numbers but has a problem with subtracting double-digit numbers and does not seem to grasp the concept of borrowing. I will be sending additional work home with her because the extra practice should help.

Needs Practice (continued)

Double-digit subtraction, especially if there is borrowing (or other skill), seems to be presenting a difficult challenge for _____. I will be sending home extra homework to help him improve this skill.

_____ seems to enjoy learning to graph and read charts. She needs a little more practice to ensure that her graphs are accurate.

Although _____ is very good at collecting accurate data, he is having a difficult time turning the information he has collected into a graph. I will be working with him in class as well as giving him some extra graphing activities to bring home. It would be helpful if you could do them together.

_____ understands the concept of single-digit division but has not learned the basic division facts, so her answers are often wrong. It would be helpful to _____ if you could work with her to practice her basic division facts.

_____ is having trouble with double-digit division and needs a lot of practice. I will be working with him in class as well as sending extra work home. Please help make sure he does the extra work.

I am very pleased with _____'s written math work. He has a difficult time, however, communicating his work orally. He clearly knows which concepts or rules to apply, but he is unable to verbalize the information. It might be helpful if he could spend time telling you what we are doing in math. If he speaks only in general terms, ask if he could explain it to you by walking you through a problem we did in class. I believe _____ will benefit by discussing math in a situation where he is more comfortable.

Struggling

Math is not _____'s favorite subject, and it seems she is having a hard time concentrating and staying on task during math.

_____ does well with higher-level problem solving skills but cannot seem to master the basic facts. He needs to practice these facts at home.

16

Struggling (continued)

_____ is struggling to keep up and stay on grade level. I think he would benefit from doing extra work at home every night. I will call you to discuss what we can do to help _____ keep up and hopefully get ahead.

_____ has mastered the basic facts but is having a difficult time tackling more complex concepts. She needs to remember to break the more difficult problems into smaller steps, instead of trying to attack them as a whole.

_____ does not seem to be putting forth his best effort when it comes to math. I really feel he could do better in math and think that if we encourage him both in school and at home his work will improve.

_____ does a great job adding any single digits, and can even add a column of single digits, but she has trouble adding double-digit numbers and does not seem to be able to grasp the concept of carrying at this time. We are working on this in class, and I will be sending home some extra practice.

_____ tries hard, but his math work is very inconsistent. I am somewhat concerned about his overall progress. I will be calling you to discuss _____'s work and to see if we can find ways to help him.

I am concerned that if _____ does not apply herself she is going to be left behind in math. We are finishing up with double-digit subtraction with borrowing (or other skill) and will be moving on to multiplication (or other skill) soon, and _____ is not ready. I am going to be sending home extra math work every night to help her catch up.

Attitude

_____ has a good attitude toward math but is progressing slowly and needs to practice his multiplication tables (or other skill) in order to keep up with his class work.

_____'s attitude toward math needs improvement. Perhaps you could take advantage of opportunities at home to point out how math is used every day.

Math

Attitude (continued)

_____ feels that she is not good at math and therefore is not putting forth an effort to improve her work. Please encourage her to try her best.

_____ does not seem to be interested in math and frequently talks and disrupts others during math class. I would like to arrange a conference to discuss a plan for getting _____ back on track.

Careless Work

_____ needs to work on her neatness. Her math problems are often done wrong simply because she is not lining up her work properly. I suggest that she try doing her math work on graph paper in order to help her organize the problems.

_____ understands math concepts and knows what to do, but he is careless so his accuracy often suffers. If he learns to work more slowly and carefully, I believe his accuracy will immediately improve.

_____ has excellent computation skills but her accuracy suffers because she does not go back and check her work.

Science

Science teaches students about processes that can be applied to other areas. This is one curriculum area from which parents often shy away. You have a much better chance of getting parents involved if they understand how important science is to their child's academic success.

Succeeding or Improving

I was pleased with _____'s overall approach and achievements in science this grading period. She stayed focused during class and lab activities, and consistently strove to do her very best.

_____'s homework assignments and lab reports exhibited a truly conscientious effort and they showed a genuine grasp of the material.

Although _____ often works too quickly and is at times impatient during science experiments, I must say that overall he demonstrates a good command of the concepts and facts that we covered this grading period.

_____ really seems to enjoy science. She is always willing to participate and to help with experiments. She works well with others in a lab setting. I am very pleased to have her in my science class.

It is a real pleasure having _____ in science class. He seems to have a real aptitude for science. I hope to encourage him to do his best and to continue his science interests outside the classroom.

_____ seems to really enjoy the magic of discovering the mysteries of science. She has an inquisitive mind, which I hope she never loses. It is really a pleasure to have her in science class.

_____ has great leadership skills. He seems to naturally take the lead in most of the labs that are assigned, and he is a positive influence. He makes sure all members participate and tries to make all of them feel that they are a part of the group. His group generally does the best lab work. I think the other students look up to him. _____ is born leader and an excellent science student.

Succeeding or Improving (continued)

I know that science class has been a real challenge for _____ this year, with its written work, lab work, research, and readings. I believe, however, that it has been a very positive experience for her and should help her succeed in future studies.

I am very proud of _____'s efforts to improve his science grade this quarter. He has turned in every homework assignment and has increased his participation in class. Please encourage him to keep up the good work.

Struggling

_____ tries very hard in science class, but he is struggling just to grasp basic concepts. I would like to get a peer tutor for him (or other outside help). I believe this will really help him get back on track.

_____ needs to work on her observation skills. She has trouble deciding what parts of the things she sees are important and should be recorded in her data book. Perhaps you could sprout a lima bean or some other plant at home and _____ could practice recording daily observations in her data book.

_____ is having a difficult time learning about the food pyramid (or other skill). I am sending home some extra material on this topic, and I would appreciate it if you could help him study this information. Perhaps you could look at the foods in your refrigerator or pantry and discuss where they belong on the food pyramid (or other activity).

We have been doing a variety of activities in class to help students increase their observation skills. Every student has a data book in which to record observations. _____ has been struggling with this assignment. Some extra practice at home may help her with her science work. For example, when you are driving in the car, you could ask _____ to look at a scene and then close her eyes and tell you everything she saw (or other activity).

_____ is having trouble recording data on a graph. I will be asking him to do some extra activities in class as well as at home. It would helpful if you could review his science homework before he turns it in.

Struggling (continued)

The scientific method seems to be a real challenge for _____. Writing a hypothesis (or other step) seems to be the biggest stumbling block. Please encourage him to continue to give his best effort, and I am sure with practice he will master this skill.

_____ is having a difficult time verbalizing her thoughts and observations in science. She does a wonderful job writing them but has a hard time, even in a small group, sharing them orally. We will be spending more time on oral presentations, as everyone could use the practice. I believe with time and practice, _____'s oral presentation skills will improve. Perhaps she could practice at home by telling you about what she has been observing and doing in science each week.

I know _____ has done all of the science labs that have been assigned, but to date he has not written up any of them or turned in a lab book. I have asked him about them several times and he assures me they are being done. I think it would be helpful if you and I had a phone conference to discuss the situation.

I am concerned because _____ has missed several science assignments this quarter. She cannot continue to miss assignments and do well in class. I will be sending you a list of the assignments and their due dates. If possible, please make sure she turns in all work on time.

_____ has a positive attitude toward science and clearly gives his best effort, although he is struggling to keep up. He is going to need all of the help and support we can give. I will be sending home some extra activities that I think will help, and I would also like to get a peer tutor for him.

Attitude and Behavior

_____ is an active participant in class when she can refer to her prepared assignments but not when we discuss new material. _____ is really very good in science. I would like to see her get more involved in discussions that initiate new topics.

_____ is very unsure of himself in science class and is hesitant to participate in experiments. In order to help build his self-confidence, I will give him some simple experiments to do at home. It would help _____ succeed if you would make sure he does each experiment and records all observations in his lab book.

Attitude and Behavior (continued)

I am concerned because _____ does not always practice safety in science class. She consistently needs to be reminded to wear her safety goggles and to use safety gloves. I always keep a close eye on her during lab, and I hope that you will help me convince _____ of the importance of safety in the lab.

_____ likes to play and joke around during our science experiments, which is disruptive and can be dangerous. I have talked to him about it several times. I would like to meet with you to discuss this problem and together try to find ways to help _____ settle down.

_____ enjoys participating in science experiments and has a good understanding of the concepts we are studying. I am concerned that she tends to play with the materials in the lab. I have explained to her that this can be very dangerous and that she must take more care if she wants to continue to participate.

_____ is doing well in science. She works well independently and is making an effort to do her best. She is having trouble, however, getting along with other students in lab. I will be working with _____ to encourage her to develop a positive working relationship with her classmates in lab.

Science labs offer children a wonderful opportunity to explore the world around them, as well an opportunity to develop connections with their peers. _____ tends to sit back and let others in the group conduct the experiments. I hope that, with more time and experience, _____ will develop more confidence and will become a contributing member of his lab group. I will be spending extra time working with his group, encouraging them to include _____, and helping them learn to work as a team.

_____ is doing well in science. Recently, however, we have been examining a variety of objects under a microscope (or other activity). She could not close one eye and focus the microscope (or other fine motor skill). I wanted you to be aware of this. Although I believe she will develop the fine motor skills necessary to use a microscope if given time, right now it is quite frustrating for her. If she is still unable to use a microscope after a few months, we should get together and discuss the situation.

Science is not _____'s favorite class. While he excels in most other classes, he is struggling in science. I believe if we could get him excited about what we are doing in class, he would easily succeed. Perhaps a trip to a museum of science would spark some excitement.

Attitude and Behavior (continued)

_____ does excellent written and lab work. He begins his experiment, makes his observations, analyzes and records the data, and hypothesizes on the possible outcomes, but will not take an educated guess on what the outcome might be. He seems very concerned about being wrong. I have encouraged him not to worry about being wrong, but so far I have not had a lot of success. I will be pushing him to take some chances and to make some educated guesses as we move forward.

We have spent a lot of time in class on activities that show students how to work through the scientific process, but _____ is always in a rush. She tends to jump to conclusions quickly instead of taking her time, analyzing the data she has collected, and working through to the conclusion. I will be trying to help her slow down and use the information she has collected.

_____ does not seem to like science. I believe she is going to need all of the encouragement she can get, both at school and at home, if she is going to do well. It would help if you could take opportunities as they present themselves to explain how science is used in our everyday lives. For example, I know _____ likes to bake, so you might talk about the science of yeast making dough rise (or other activity).

Informing Parents of Class Activities

We will be doing experiments on texture and taste soon. The class will be eating a variety of foods and recording their impressions of each. If _____ has any food allergies, please fill out and return the enclosed form. You could help _____ with this project if you would discuss the foods you eat at dinner and let him try to express what their textures and tastes are like.

We have been studying food and nutrition. I have asked each student to keep a diary of all of the foods she eats and to categorize the foods into the basic food groups. If you talked about what foods you eat at dinner and in what groups they belong, it would help _____ gain a better understanding.

We are going to be exploring sound (or other topic) over the next few weeks. I will be asking each student to keep a diary of the sounds he hears (or other activity). It would be beneficial if you could review it a couple of times a week and make sure _____ writes daily entries.

Informing Parents of Class Activities (continued)

We will be studying simple machines (or other topic) soon. I will be sending home activities for each student to do at home. The activities will include simple experiments using levers or pulleys (or other activities). It would be very helpful if _____ could demonstrate the activities for you once she masters them.

Science Fair time is just around the corner. It would be great if you could help _____ think of some ideas for his Science Fair project. Perhaps a little research at the library or on the Internet would spark some creative ideas.

We will be exploring the environment (or other topic) over the next month. I will ask each child to pick an area of interest and write a research paper. Students will be expected not only to do research on the Internet but also to go to the library. I will be sending home a sheet listing all of the steps and due dates. Please help _____ get organized at home and adhere to this schedule. If you have any questions regarding the schedule and what is expected, please call me.

I wanted you to know that the first unit we will be doing during the next grading period will be exploring the effects of drugs and alcohol on the human body. I think it is very important that students clearly understand the effect drugs and alcohol can have on their bodies, brains, and overall development. If you have any questions regarding this unit, please call me.

Social Studies

If we can help our students become curious about the world and respectful of other peoples and cultures, we will have helped our students take the first step to becoming citizens of the world.

Succeeding or Improving

I am very pleased with _____'s progress in social studies. We have been studying our government (or other topic) and _____ has willingly volunteered his thoughts and participated in all the activities we have been doing.

_____ has done a wonderful job keeping the class up-to-date on current events. I want to thank you for the help you have given _____ and to thank him for his efforts. He has helped the entire class by bringing world events into our room.

_____ loves geography (or other topic). She seems to have a good understanding of the topic and enjoys studying it.

_____ seems to have a gift for studying history (or other topic). He loves it and seems to have a real grasp of how and why world events affect political decisions (or other topic). _____ is doing very well in this subject area and should be encouraged to do more outside reading in history.

We studied our state (or other topic) this grading period, and I was pleased with _____'s overall approach to the assignments and projects. She did very well and really put forth a great effort.

_____ puts a tremendous amount of effort into his social studies work. It appears that social studies is his favorite class. He never misses a project or assignment and is always willing to do extra credit work. It is really a joy to have _____ in this class.

I know social studies is not _____'s favorite subject, so I am pleased that we have found an area in which she seems to find both enjoyment and success. _____ really enjoys studying maps (or other topic). I am happy to tell you that _____ has really excelled during recent weeks. Please encourage her to keep up the good work.

Social Studies

Struggling

_____ is having a difficult time memorizing the information we are studying about states and capitals (or other topic). I believe he is having a problem organizing the material in such a way that he can study this much at once. We have talked about some study tips that I hope will help. It may also be helpful if you could make sure he has a quiet, neat study area at home where he can work undisturbed.

_____ is having a hard time learning how to read maps (or other skill). I will be giving her some mapping activities and worksheets to do at home. If you have some time and could help her with the worksheets, it might be very beneficial.

_____ is having a hard time with the concept of north, south, east, and west (or other skill). I have been doing a variety of mapping activities to help all the students, but _____ seems to be having a particularly difficult time. I think that, after working through some extra activities and assignments, he will do fine. If not, I will call you so we can discuss some ways to help him.

_____ does not seem to be giving her best effort in social studies, although she is doing fine in other subject areas. I have spoken with her on several occasions with little result. I think we should talk; I will call you next week to set up a time for a conference. I look forward to discussing this with you and seeing what we can do to improve _____'s work.

_____ is having a difficult time with social studies. Keeping dates and events straight (or other skill) seems to be a special challenge for him. _____ is going to have to give his best effort, both in school and studying at home, if he is going to be successful in this subject.

I am concerned because _____ has not yet picked a topic for his social studies paper. The paper is an important part of this class. It must be turned in by _____ . If he cannot find a topic of interest, then he is welcome to pick one from the list of ideas that I provided. Perhaps you could go over the list with him and help him pick a topic.

_____ has been working hard and has made some big improvements on her mapping skills, but she still needs to work on the concept of scale (or other skill). We will be doing more activities in class to reinforce this skill, but I think she is going to need some extra help. I will be sending home some activities and worksheets for her to do. It would be helpful if you could go over them with her once she has done them.

26

Struggling (continued)

We have been studying basic economics and looking at supply and demand (or other topic). This can be a hard concept for students to grasp. I know _____ is frustrated, and I have been spending extra time with her. I will also get her a peer tutor. I think these extra steps will help.

We are studying the three branches of government (or other topic), and _____ is having a difficult time keeping the legislative, judicial, and executive branches separate (or other skill). He needs to spend more time taking notes and studying them if he is going to learn the information.

Attitude and Behavior

I feel that _____ does not think that social studies is an important class. Her poor attitude is being reflected in the quality of her work and the inconsistency with which she is doing the assignments. I would like to discuss this with you at your convenience.

We spent much of this grading period looking at world history (or other topic). This did not appear to be _____'s favorite subject area, and he did not seem to put forth his best effort. I have spoken with him and he knows I expect to see an improvement soon.

We studied our state (or other topic) this month, and I was disappointed with the effort _____ put forth. He only participated when called upon and did only the bare minimum to get by. _____ and I have discussed his performance, and he has assured me he will work harder in the future.

_____ has no problem doing any assignment that only uses our textbook. When any other reference material is required, however, he does not usually do the assignment. I have discussed this with _____ and have explained I expect him to do all the assignments, including the ones that require a trip to the library or using the Internet in the computer lab.

We have been studying other cultures and their contributions (or other topic). At the end of the unit, each student gave an oral report. _____ was very concerned about the oral presentation. She had a difficult time talking in front of the class. We will be doing more oral presentations during the year, so it might be helpful if you encourage _____ to practice several times in front of a mirror and then in front of you before her next presentation.

Social Studies

Attitude and Behavior (continued)

_____ seems to be struggling to learn the different geographic regions of the United States (or other topic). I believe she could learn this without a problem, but for some reason she just is not applying herself. I am going to give her some assignments to do at home in this area. It would be helpful if you could work with her on these assignments.

We spent much of this month studying the continents (or other topic) and each student did a project to present in class. I feel that _____ put very little effort into her project. I have asked her to redo the project and have given her two weeks (or other deadline). It would be helpful if you read the instructions she was given and make sure she does the project. Please call me if you have any questions.

I am concerned that _____ is having some problems in social studies class. He has a hard time taking turns and tends to interrupt others while they are talking. I will be working with him to improve these skills, and I thought it was important that you be aware of the situation. I think it would help if you would talk to _____ about what is happening.

_____ seems to spend too much time socializing in class, rather than paying attention and learning about history. I have explained to _____ that if he is going to be successful in this class he will have to give it his full attention.

Informing Parents of Class Activities

Our class is going to be studying holidays around the world, and we are planning to celebrate several of them in the classroom. I am asking students and parents to volunteer to make decorations and cook various foods. If you wish to volunteer to decorate or cook for one of the holidays, please call me at your earliest convenience.

We are going to be studying _____ (topic) soon. There are going to be several wonderful programs about this topic on television. I will be sending home a list telling you when these programs will air and on what networks. I think it would be very helpful for _____ to see them.

We spent part of this month exploring various careers and career opportunities. I think _____ really enjoyed looking at different types of jobs. He seems very taken with the idea of being a chef (or other career). I suggested that he might want to use the Internet or go to the library to research what this type of work would entail.

Computer Skills

Computers are a part of our everyday life. Although there may not be a computer in every home, a child who does not have adequate computer skills will be at a disadvantage. Parents need to understand that as their children grow up computer skills will be as necessary as reading and writing skills.

Succeeding or Improving

Computer class is clearly _____'s favorite class. He has shown a real talent for computers and has even done some basic beginning programming. To encourage him to develop this talent to its fullest potential, I will schedule _____ for extra time in the computer lab.

_____ has excellent computer skills and really enjoys working and exploring on the computer. I would encourage you to see if there are any computer classes outside of school that might be available to her.

_____ loves using the computer. His keyboarding skills could use a little work, but his overall computer knowledge is very strong. He can navigate the Internet better than most students his age. I am concerned, however, because he seems to find all his information for class on the Internet. I think it is important for him to be able to use other sources as well. The next time he has to find some facts I am going to ask him to do it without using a computer.

_____ has wonderful computer skills. Sometimes I am concerned, however, because she seems to prefer the computer to the company of other people. I would like to make her a computer buddy. She will be paired with another student who needs help on the computer. _____ will share her computer skills with her buddy. This could help her form relationships with her classmates.

Struggling

_____ loves using the computer. He can use the Internet to find whatever information he is seeking. His keyboarding skills, however, are weak. I will make sure _____ practices on some of the typing programs we have here at school. Perhaps they will help him get on the right track with a keyboard.

Struggling (continued)

_____ enjoys using the computer, has good basic keyboarding skills, and knows a few basic programs. He has rarely been on-line, however, and would benefit from more time spent learning how to navigate the Internet.

_____ has excellent keyboarding skills, but I believe his penmanship is suffering because he tries to use the computer exclusively and almost never writes anything by hand. I am going to ask _____ to limit himself to doing about half of his written work on the computer and the other half by hand.

_____ seems to know very little about the computer. I am going to arrange for her to have a computer buddy at school. Her buddy will show her how to use the basic programs and how to use the Internet. If you have a computer at home, you could encourage _____ to practice using it. Computers are also available for use at the local library.

_____ appears to be a bit intimidated by computers and is not always sure what to do with them. If you have access to a computer, he may benefit from spending some time on it just to help build his self-confidence.

Art & Music

Studies have proven that music can help children develop higher-level thinking skills. Art can help children develop a better self-image. Art and music are both important to the development of the whole child. For some children, these will be the only subject areas in which they may excel.

Art

_____'s scissors skills are excellent. She loves to color, cut, and paste. It is fun to watch her create. She really seems to love art class.

Making collages (or other project) seems to be _____'s favorite thing to do in art class lately. Give him some scissors, paper, and glue, and he will create a masterpiece. It is a joy to watch him in class. I hope he will have as much enthusiasm for his other classes as he grows.

_____ takes real pride in her artwork and really seems to enjoy it. She also takes excellent care of her supplies and always cleans up when done.

_____ loves to draw and appears to be very talented. He is always drawing in his notebooks. You might consider getting him a sketch pad and a small set of drawing pencils to encourage his talent.

_____ really seems to enjoy art class. He loves looking at pictures and talking about them as much as drawing with his markers. It would be wonderful if you had an opportunity to take him to an art museum.

The students have been exploring different art mediums, working with watercolors, clay, oils, charcoals, etc. _____ has shown an incredible talent for working with clay (or other medium). Her work is exceptional for her age and she should be encouraged to pursue her talents.

_____ has a real talent for art. He has a natural understanding of light and shadow and works well with any medium, but has a particular love of charcoals and pastels (or other medium).

_____ loves art class and eagerly participates. Unfortunately, she never wants to help clean up at the end of class. We have discussed this and she knows that if she is going to participate she must help clean up at the end.

Art (continued)

_____'s scissors skills are not quite as strong as they should be. I do not think there is any reason to worry. His fine motor skills just need to develop a little more. It may be helpful if you encourage him to cut out pictures at home.

_____ seems to enjoy art but has trouble completing her projects. This has become very frustrating for her. I believe it would be good for her if you would encourage her to complete unfinished work at home. Hopefully this will give her a better sense of accomplishment.

Music

_____ loves music class. She really listens and gets involved in whatever piece of music is playing. It is a joy to watch her. I hope she never loses this love of music.

_____ loves to sing. He has a good strong voice for his age and can really carry a tune. I would encourage him to try out for the choir next year.

_____ is doing well in music class. She can recognize all the parts of the orchestra and knows what instruments make up the brass, percussion, string, and woodwind sections.

We have been listening to various types of music from all over the world. _____ is clearly developing a deep appreciation for all types of music, which seems to be stimulating curiosity about other cultures.

_____ seems to have a real aptitude for music and is interested in playing an instrument. He can recognize many instruments by sound, is able to read notes, and can identify simple forms of music. I would encourage him to play an instrument if he continues to be interested.

_____ has a difficult time sitting still and listening in music class. She tends to talk to her neighbor and generally disrupt the class. We have talked about her behavior, and I will watch it over the next few weeks. I will call you if there is no improvement.

_____ does not seem interested in music class and often has a difficult time paying attention. We have discussed this and he seems to be trying harder, but music is not his favorite class.

Physical Education

Physical education is important to our children for many reasons. It is important that parents understand that there are many skills their children will learn in physical education, not the least of which are sportsmanship, coordination, motor skills, spatial awareness, and cooperative play.

Succeeding or Improving

_____ is not always the strongest athlete in the class, but she is always willing to participate and sets a wonderful example for the rest of the class.

_____ is always a good team member and is willing to play on any team to which he is assigned. It is a pleasure having him in class.

_____ has learned to be a great team member. She is supportive of her fellow players and is a good sport whether they win or not. It has been a pleasure to watch her grow and mature.

_____ is a very talented athlete. He is a born captain and a leader. He is also a wonderful sportsman and sets an excellent example for his fellow teammates.

Physical education class has been very good for _____ this year. Her motor skills have improved dramatically. You should be very pleased with her progress.

_____ has really benefited from his physical education classes this year. He has developed great sportsmanship skills. He truly seems to understand that it is important to take turns and that he cannot always win. You can be very proud of his progress.

_____ is a very good athlete. Currently, however, she is struggling with some of her academic studies. Given the academic problems she is experiencing, sports have become an important way for _____ to help build and support her self-confidence.

_____ is in much better physical shape than he was at the beginning of the year. He really enjoys playing team sports now and seems to be excelling at softball (or other sport), which has been great for his self-confidence as well.

Physical Education

Developmental Concerns

_____ is struggling in physical education. At present, she demonstrates weak motor skills and poor hand-to-eye coordination. As she matures and plays more sports, both of these areas should improve dramatically.

_____ should be encouraged to participate in more outdoor activities and team sports. His coordination is a little weak and playing more outdoor games may help him develop these skills.

_____ has been having a difficult time in physical education of late. She has gone through a growth spurt and her coordination has not caught up with her height yet. When team sports are played she is often picked last, which can be very hurtful. I think it is important that we meet to discuss this situation.

Behavioral Concerns

_____ would really benefit from participating in a team sport on a regular basis. He has a hard time taking turns and can show poor sportsmanship. If he played on a team regularly, it might help him develop these skills.

_____ does not seem to enjoy gym class and often refuses to participate. I would like to talk to you about the situation. Any insights you may have would be appreciated.

_____ says she enjoys gym class and looks forward to it. Yet she often acts out until she is asked to leave the class. I would like to talk to you about the situation and would appreciate any suggestions you may have.

_____ knows that suitable clothing and proper shoes are both required in order to participate in gym class. Although it is his responsibility to remember them, perhaps you could help him find ways to carry out this responsibility.

_____ often chooses to wear a dress on gym days. If she wears a dress, she needs to wear shorts under it. If you have any questions about this, please feel free to call me.

Behavioral Concerns (continued)

_____ never seems to remember to bring his gym clothes on P.E. day. Perhaps you could help him remember to bring them on _____ (day).

_____ is a good athlete. She is often not happy playing on a team, however, unless she is the captain. In gym class, everyone gets a chance to be captain no matter how weak or strong an athlete he or she is. Please help me to encourage _____ to be more of a team player.

_____ tends to take our gym class a little too seriously. He has very little patience for weaker athletes. We have emphasized that in our class we are only "playing for fun." _____ has a difficult time with this concept, as he always plays to win. You might want to discuss his feelings with him and encourage him continue to do his best, but to have more patience with his teammates.

Work/Study Habits

Good organization and study skills take time to develop but are certainly worth the time. By learning positive work habits and utilizing good study strategies, a student will be well-served throughout his entire life.

Listening/Following Directions

_____ is an excellent student capable of grasping even the most complex directions in either a written or an oral format. He is a delight to have in class and does very well in school!

_____ does quite well in her schoolwork and is a very good listener. She follows directions well and pays attention in class.

_____ could benefit from working a little harder on his listening skills. He is easily distracted and therefore, at times, does not listen to or follow all of the directions being given.

_____ is having a difficult time following a series of directions. I am a little concerned about this and would like to set up a phone conference with you or schedule a meeting to discuss some suggestions for helping her.

_____ seems to have a hard time following oral directions, especially if there are two or more directions. Perhaps working on this at home might help. Give _____ a series of directions and help him think them through, coaching if necessary. For example, "Please go to the living room, get the house keys, and return them to our key rack." You might want to approach this as a fun game with both you and your child taking turns giving directions.

_____ is very creative but doesn't seem to like to follow specific directions. She prefers to do assignments her own way. We have discussed this several times in class, and although I'm not extremely concerned at this time, I did want to make you aware of the situation.

Written instructions seem to present a real challenge to _____. He seems to have a difficult time understanding directions that have multiple steps. Perhaps we could arrange a time later this week to discuss some ways to help _____ improve this skill.

Class Work

_____ is a pleasure to have in class. She works hard and uses her time wisely to complete her class work accurately. She sets an excellent example for the other students.

_____ really takes an interest in his schoolwork and is eager to participate in class activities. He is a creative thinker, and he regularly shares his thoughts and ideas with the class during discussions.

_____ seems to enjoy class but never raises her hand or participates voluntarily. We have discussed this, and I have encouraged her to join in class activities and discussions. If you have any suggestions, I would appreciate talking with you.

_____ seems to do his best work in a quiet environment which is free of distractions. The quality of _____'s class work has improved dramatically since he started to use an individual study carrel when doing independent assignments. Encourage him to keep up the good work.

_____ is doing a good job academically this grading period, but she needs to improve the speed with which she does most assignments. She tends to work very slowly and generally does not finish an assignment within the allotted time. We have talked about her need to push a little harder and try to work faster.

_____ is trying very hard in school but he rushes through assignments and tends to make careless errors. We have discussed the fact that he needs to slow down, work more carefully, and check his work before turning it in.

Homework

_____ consistently turns in complete and accurate homework assignments. He is a very responsible student.

_____ is a cooperative and hard-working student. She completes all of her homework assignments and is always prepared for class discussions and tests.

Homework (continued)

It appears _____ has a difficult time remembering all of his homework assignments. Perhaps it would help if he had a special notebook in which to write them down. Reviewing each assignment with him and making sure he understands all the directions before he starts may also be helpful.

Getting ready to complete assignments appears to be hard for _____. It might be helpful if you help her make sure she is prepared with assignment information, books, paper, pencil, etc., when it is time for her to do homework. A quiet place to work at home with good lighting would also help.

_____ often forgets and leaves the books he will need to do his homework at school. I have developed an assignment sheet which requires him to list his assignments and which books he will need to complete each one. If you could review this sheet with _____ and make sure he has all the books he will need, it may help him get organized.

_____ is working hard in school. However, she seems to be having difficulty completing her homework assignments correctly. Perhaps it would help if you could review each homework assignment with her before she begins and set a schedule to complete her homework at the same time each day.

It appears that _____'s attitude toward his homework assignments seems to be shifting toward thinking that they do not matter. It is important that he gives them his best effort. Perhaps if you review them nightly and reinforce their importance, _____ will get back on track.

_____ is easily distracted while studying. It might be helpful if you could make sure that she has a quiet place to work that is free of distractions when doing assignments at home.

_____ needs to work on developing good study habits. We are making a checklist so he has everything he needs to do his work and to work efficiently when it is time to study or do homework. If you could post this list where _____ does his work at home it would be very helpful.

I am concerned that _____'s poor grades this quarter are due to her incomplete homework assignments. When she does not do her homework, she is not prepared for the next day's lesson, and ends up falling behind. I would like to talk with you about this, and perhaps together we can think of some ways to help _____.

Organization

_____ has excellent organizational skills. She is always ready with the proper materials and keeps her papers and work area neat and orderly.

_____ is a very responsible and organized student. He keeps track of his assignments and turns them in when they are due.

_____ has trouble keeping his desk neat. This leads to lost items and disorganized work, in addition to looking messy. I will work with him to help him develop better organizational skills.

_____ needs to work on developing her organizational skills. She can seldom find anything in her desk or backpack, and she often forgets to do assignments. It might be helpful if you get _____ a student organizer or calendar in which she can write all her homework assignments and keep track of her schedule.

Attendance/Tardiness

Attendance is important if a child is going to grasp all of the sequential concepts being taught and develop to the best of her ability.

You can be very proud of _____, as he has had perfect attendance so far this year.

_____ has not missed a single day of school so far this year. This has helped her progress more quickly academically. Encourage her to keep up the good work!

_____'s attendance improved greatly this grading period. Thank you for your efforts.

It is very encouraging that _____'s attendance is improving. His schoolwork also seems to be showing improvement. Please continue to help _____ stay on this track.

_____'s tardiness is becoming a problem. It seems to be getting worse. At first, she was late once or twice a month. Now she is late once or twice a week. It is important that she make a greater effort to get to school on time.

_____ is late for school at least once a week. This seems to be affecting his work, as he has a hard time settling down to work on those days. It is also disruptive for the rest of the class.

Up until this grading period, _____ had perfect attendance. Now she is absent almost once a week. Is there something going on with _____ that we should talk about?

_____ has been absent so much this grading period that it has really started to affect his schoolwork. He is falling behind in both math and reading (or other subjects). I think we should talk about the situation.

_____ will be missing a fair amount of work while you are on vacation. I would like to suggest that she take along some work so she does not fall too far behind while you are away.

_____ has missed a significant amount of school because of his recent illness. I know this could not be avoided, but I think we need to talk about how we are going to help _____ make the transition back to school. He has a lot of work to make up, and I want to be sure he does not get frustrated trying to do too much too quickly. I will call you to set up a time to talk.

Attitude

Teachers know that attitude can make a huge difference. In fact, for many students, it can be the difference between success and failure. A student can be highly intelligent, but if she has a poor attitude she will not achieve her personal best.

Positive Attitude

_____ is a delight in class and has a wonderful attitude toward his schoolwork as well as his extracurricular activities. He always gives his best effort and keeps a positive attitude, which often helps the entire class or team.

_____'s positive attitude toward her work has been critical to her success. The improvement in her grades is proof of the importance of attitude and how it can affect a student's achievement.

_____ has a wonderful attitude toward school. It is truly a pleasure to watch him settle down and get to work. I am pleased that he feels hard work and a positive attitude are such an important part of succeeding in school.

_____'s optimism and positive attitude are absolutely infectious. They really help her achieve her personal best and motivate many of her fellow classmates to try harder.

_____ takes great pride in her schoolwork and in her classroom jobs. She has a terrific attitude about school and learning that I hope will continue throughout her school career.

Needs Improvement

Although _____ has made some improvements in her attitude toward others, she still needs work in this area. This is especially true in the area of sportsmanship and overall respect for her fellow students. We have discussed this several times and are working on strategies that may help her forge better relationships with her peers.

There are times when _____ seems to know he is going to have a bad day. His attitude reflects these feelings, and it becomes difficult for him to settle down and get any work done. We have discussed this several times and are working on strategies that may help him. I would like you to be involved in this process. Please call me to schedule an appointment.

Attitude

Needs Improvement (continued)

Although there have been some improvements in _____'s attitude toward her schoolwork, they have not been very consistent. I think we should talk, and I would appreciate any insights you may have.

_____'s attitude toward school rules is of concern. He consistently disregards them and has become increasingly hostile this grading period. I would appreciate talking with you about any insights you may have.

_____ has gained a lot of self-confidence this year, but her attitude could still use a boost. When she is afraid of failing, her attitude reflects it. We have discussed this several times and are working on strategies that may help her.

Although _____ has improved his attitude toward his peers, he will continue to need our support and encouragement to forge better relationships with his classmates.

_____'s negative attitude toward his homework assignments seems to be affecting his work. He has missed several assignments, and the quality of the homework he is doing has gone down significantly. Perhaps you can review his assignments nightly.

_____'s report card is really a reflection of her effort and attitude in school these days. There is no doubt she could do better. To succeed she needs to improve both her effort and attitude.

_____ needs to improve her attitude in school. She has a difficult time accepting authority and tends to become very angry if corrected in any way. We have discussed this and are working on strategies that may help.

It is of concern that recently _____'s attitude toward school has changed dramatically. I am really not sure why, and I would appreciate any insights you may have.

_____'s attitude toward his schoolwork needs to improve if he is going to be successful this year. Encouragement and support here at school do not seem to be making as big a difference as hoped. I will call you to set up a conference. Perhaps together we can help _____ work on this.

Classroom Behavior

A good learning environment is important for successful teaching. Student behavior can be one of a teacher's biggest challenges and one of the hardest things to communicate to parents and guardians.

Positive Behavior

_____'s behavior is always exemplary. He is truly a delight, and I love having him in class.

_____ has really settled down this grading period. Her conduct has improved, and her academic work is also showing signs of improvement. It would be wonderful if this trend continues throughout the rest of the year.

_____ has excellent manners, which seem to be extending to his peer group. It is a pleasure to listen to him in a small group, as he always says please, thank you, or excuse me. He sets a great example for other students.

It is really a joy to have _____ in class. She is always well-behaved and has excellent manners. She sets an excellent example for her fellow students.

Noise and Disruptions

_____ has a difficult time settling down to work in the morning. He is very social and would rather talk with friends than work on assignments. _____ and I have been talking about this and trying to find ways to solve the problem.

I enjoy having _____ in class. She is bright, outgoing, and lots of fun. She has a hard time, however, working quietly. She likes making people laugh, and would prefer to do that than just about anything else. I encourage you to sign her up for drama or another activity that might offer an outlet for her wonderful sense of humor. In the meantime, I will continue to work toward having her do her tasks quietly in class.

_____ has a difficult time working quietly at his desk. He always seems to want to talk to his neighbors and disturb them. We have talked about his need to exercise more self-control. I have seen some improvement, but he still has a lot of work to do.

Classroom Behavior

Noise and Disruptions (continued)

_____ had a difficult time settling back into the school routine after vacation. She tried very hard and eventually got back on track. Hopefully this will be easier after our next break.

_____ can be disruptive in class when he finishes an assignment and has some free time. He needs to develop a little more self-control and be more responsible for himself. He and I have been working on some ideas that should help.

_____ has difficulty making the transition from our classroom to the library (or other area). Please help me remind her to keep her hands to herself and that classroom behavior is still required in the hallways and other areas of the school.

Not Following Class Rules

_____ often does not follow our classroom rules. He and I have discussed this several times. He seems to have a difficult time with self-control. Although this may be more of a maturity issue than anything else, he knows he still needs to try harder to work within our class rules.

I am concerned that _____ does not always seem able to conduct herself as expected in class. We have discussed her conduct many times, and now I feel it is necessary for you and me to talk. I will call you to set up a conference. Any insights you may have would be welcome.

_____ seems to have a great deal of difficulty with any kind of authority. This is affecting his work as well as his relationships with other students. I think we should set up a conference to discuss the situation. Any suggestions you may be able to offer would be appreciated.

_____'s classroom behavior is very inconsistent. She seems to have a difficult time with following rules. I will call you this week to set up a conference to discuss how we can help her remember and follow our class rules.

_____ is having trouble remembering to follow our class rules. I am sending home a copy of the rules, and it would help _____ if you would review them with him. Thank you for your help.

Manners

_____ needs to work on his classroom manners. He often interrupts other students and forgets to say please and thank you. We have talked about his behavior and he understands that he needs to make a greater effort in the future.

_____ has a difficult time following our class rules, especially when it comes to being polite to other students. We have been discussing the importance of manners in general. It may be helpful if you could discuss this with her at home as well.

_____ needs to work on his classroom manners. Whenever we have a class discussion he tends to just shout out whatever he wants to share, without raising his hand or waiting to be called on. We are working on this in class, but it may be helpful if you could discuss how important it is to let everyone share his ideas in a conversation.

_____ is having a difficult time taking turns in class. We have talked about this and are working on it in school. You might also want to talk to _____ at home about how important it is to take turns and let everyone participate.

When working in a group, _____ finds it difficult to allow other members to give their opinions. Although she often has valuable ideas, she needs to accept the contributions of others. When you are talking together at home perhaps you could reinforce the need to respect the opinions of others.

_____ has a difficult time remembering his manners when working in a group. He often gets so involved and excited about what he is doing that he interrupts his fellow students and forgets to say please or thank you. Although his enthusiasm is commendable, _____'s group manners need to improve.

Outside Behavior

Maintaining discipline outside the classroom can be a real challenge for any teacher. It can also be critical for the safety of the students.

Playground

_____ is a natural athlete and leader. It is a pleasure to watch her at play. She sets an excellent example of sportsmanship for her classmates.

_____ enjoys playing with his classmates on the playground. He plays fairly and always makes an effort to include others.

_____'s ability to work effectively in class is often affected by problems that started on the playground. He seems to get involved in many arguments and is often not a good sport. It might be helpful if you and I could meet and discuss ways we might help _____.

_____ is having a great deal of difficulty practicing self-control on the playground. The other children often do not ask _____ to join in because of her temper, which tends to upset her and make her more angry. We have discussed this several times and are working to help improve her self-control.

_____ finds it very difficult to interact fairly with other students on the playground. There have been increasing incidents of poor playground behavior recently. I think we should discuss this situation.

_____'s outside behavior is of real concern. It can cause him to be in situations in which he may be hurt. He and I have discussed this on several occasions, and he has promised to try harder. It may be helpful if you could talk with him about how important it is to follow the safety rules.

As we have discussed, _____ still finds it difficult to function well on the playground in organized games and group activities. We will continue to work on this, but I think that you and I should meet.

_____ does not seem interested in playground games or activities. I believe she would benefit from increased interaction with her peers. Perhaps you can encourage her to join an after-school program.

Playground (continued)

Once _____ gets on the playground it seems he leaves his classroom manners behind. He and I have talked about this and are working on strategies to help him remember that good manners are expected all the time.

_____ is often picked last when teams are chosen on the playground, and she often comes in from the playground in tears. I think you and I should meet to discuss this situation.

_____ is a very good student and is doing well academically. He seems very uncomfortable on the playground, however, and has a very difficult time joining in group activities. If this situation does not improve, I will call you to discuss it.

Bus/Car

_____'s bus driver has spoken to me several times regarding _____'s behavior on the bus. She often refuses to stay in her seat and has started a fight on two occasions (or specify other behavior). I think it is important that we meet to discuss this situation.

_____ seems to have a very difficult time getting to the bus after school. He stops to talk with friends and has almost missed the bus on many occasions. We have discussed the situation several times. Perhaps you could talk to him about the problems that will arise should he miss the bus.

I know _____ has recently started having problems on the bus ride to school. I am not sure exactly what is going on, but I would like to talk to you about the situation at your earliest convenience.

I have been notified that _____ has not been minding the students who serve as bus patrol on her bus. She and I have talked about the importance of being safe on the bus and respecting the students on bus patrol. I would appreciate it if you could also emphasize this to her at home.

_____ has wandered away from the after-school pick-up area on several occasions and almost missed his ride. _____ needs to understand that he must be responsible for himself both in school and after school.

Outside Behavior

Bus/Car continued

_____ has gotten into fights on several occasions (or other behavior) while waiting for her ride. She has been told to stay with the teacher on duty until her bus (or van) arrives.

_____ has left his schoolbooks on the ground in the after-school pick-up area on several occasions. Although they have been returned to our classroom, _____ has been unable to study or do his homework on those nights. He needs to try harder to remember to bring his books home.

_____ has trouble remembering that school rules still apply even after school is dismissed. She has been in a couple of fights (or other behavior) while waiting for the bus. We have talked about this, and I have explained that if her after-school behavior does not improve, you and I will have to discuss this problem.

Other

_____ seems to get very excited at the end of the school day and forget our safety rules. She tends to run rather than walk (or other behavior). _____ must take better responsibility for her actions after school. We have discussed this, and she has promised to try harder.

Having to go outside to get to another class seems to be a problem for _____. Once outside, he forgets proper school behavior. He tends to run, roughhouse, and do other inappropriate actions. We have talked about his behavior, and he has promised to improve it.

_____ has a difficult time settling down after recess or any other outdoor activity. She has trouble getting in line to come inside, and once she is in line she demonstrates little self-control. I think we should discuss the situation, and I will call you to set up a conference. Any insights you may have would be appreciated.

_____ has been having trouble being responsible when using the hall pass. He tends to take detours around the school rather than go directly to his destination and back. I have spoken with him about this several times, and I believe it would help if you could discuss it with him as well.

Character Development

Character development can be a very sensitive and subjective area of a child's development. Below are some comments that may help you better communicate with parents about a variety of areas of a child's character development.

Responsibility

_____ takes responsibly for his actions. He exhibits terrific leadership skills and sets a wonderful example for the whole class. I truly enjoy having _____ in my class.

It is really a pleasure to have _____ in class. She sets high expectations for herself and works hard to achieve them.

It has been a joy to watch _____ grow and develop this year. He is really making good, responsible choices both in and out of the classroom.

_____ has a hard time making an independent decision and taking responsibility for it. She would rather talk to her friends and make a group decision. Putting her in various situations where she must make some independent decisions may help.

When placed in a small group situation, _____ can have difficulty accepting her share of the responsibilities. It might be helpful for _____ if she were held accountable for some specific responsibilities at home.

_____ often copies the inappropriate actions of others. This is probably just a stage through which he is going, but I will keep an eye on the situation.

_____ likes to be called upon to do special class jobs, but he has a difficult time completing assigned tasks. Perhaps it would help _____ if he were given a couple of specific responsibilities at home for which he was accountable.

_____ tends to get into mischief when her work is done and there is not immediately another directed activity. She needs to work harder on taking responsibility for herself. Perhaps having a book she could read during these times would help.

Compassion

_____ is always kind to others. He empathizes with his peers and is able to work with them in almost any situation.

_____ is a very good friend and is always there to support her peers.

It is a pleasure to have _____ in class. He always has something kind to say to another student who is having a bad day.

It is nice to see that _____ really cares about other people's feelings. She is a very kind and caring person, which she consistently demonstrates through her actions and concern for her peers.

_____ is a compassionate person and is wonderful with his classmates. Other students often seek his advice when problems arise.

_____ has really contributed to the growth and maturity of his fellow students by continually setting a good example through both actions and words.

_____ would make a great peer counselor because she is such a compassionate, mature, and understanding student.

_____ is able to express his feelings well and demonstrates an unusual maturity level for his age.

_____ has a difficult time expressing her feelings, which is not uncommon at this age.

_____ has no problem expressing his feelings to others. Unfortunately, he often hurts other children's feelings, although he does not mean to, by speaking before he really thinks about what he says. I have discussed this with him already. Please talk to him about it at home as well and encourage him to consider others' feelings before he speaks.

_____ does not seem to realize how her actions might affect others. As you see situations occur at home, it would be helpful if you could talk about them and how they may affect others' feelings.

Trustworthiness and Honesty

_____ can always be counted on to tell the truth whenever she is asked a question.

It seems that if anyone loses anything, we can always count on _____ to find it and turn it into the office.

_____ is a wonderful peer advisor. He is always open and honest, and consistently gives his best effort.

I can always trust that if _____ promises to do something, she will.

_____ is a great friend to others. I have never seen her break the trust or confidence of another student.

_____ is very popular because the other students know they can count on him and can trust his word.

I can always count on _____ to give a truthful answer to any question I may ask.

_____ has a real sense of right and wrong and does not let friendships sway her beliefs. She is very mature for her age.

_____ often has a hard time admitting he is wrong. Although this is not uncommon at this age, he should be encouraged to be honest in all situations.

_____ does not like to be wrong and sometimes has problems explaining events as they actually occurred. You might want to watch for this kind of situation at home and encourage her to be factual.

_____ is not always truthful when asked about a situation. I would like to set up a conference with you to talk about this problem.

It seems _____ sometimes has a problem understanding right from wrong. I think we should meet to discuss this.

Character Development

Self-Discipline

_____ shows great self-control and always strives to work out disagreements in a positive way.

I am impressed by _____'s self-discipline. He always makes sure his work is done properly before going on to a free-time activity.

You can be very proud of _____. She sets a wonderful example for her peers and classmates and is clearly a born leader.

_____ has excellent reasoning skills and applies them well in peer situations, which helps him to make good choices.

_____ has developed good decision-making skills and is quite mature for her age.

_____ has shown great self-discipline this year. She knows what she wants and goes after it in positive ways. It is a pleasure to have her in my class.

_____ exhibits excellent self-discipline, especially for his age. He does not jump to conclusions, but instead demonstrates excellent problem-solving skills and has the ability to take the time needed to think a problem though to its logical conclusion.

_____ is an extrovert and has many friends in the school. At times it is difficult to get her to settle down and get to work. _____ and I have discussed the appropriate times for socializing and working. Reinforcing this at home with her will be appreciated.

_____ has a hard time whenever there is more than one activity going on in the room. She finds it difficult to ignore the other activities and stay on task. When _____ is doing homework it may be helpful if you could remind her to stay focused and help her stay on track until the assignment is completed.

_____ can be a little impulsive and tends to make decisions before considering the ramifications. We have discussed this several times, and over the past few weeks _____ has really made an effort to think before jumping to a decision.

Self-Discipline (continued)

I have noticed that _____ tends to have a hard time staying focused and can be easily distracted from the task at hand. It would be helpful if he had a homework routine that helped him to stay focused. A study area free of distractions would also be very helpful.

_____ seems to have a difficult time being alone and working independently. She loves working in a group. She is a wonderful group member and functions well within a group. It is important, however, that she be able to work successfully on her own. I will put her in more independent situations in class which may help.

_____ has shown a need to be the center of attention at times. I have talked to him about being more self-disciplined in class and discussed some strategies that may help.

Peer pressure can be a powerful force, and _____ seems to have a difficult time resisting it. Pairing her with students outside of her normal peer group may help. Putting her in leadership situations may also help. If neither of these strategies works, I will call you to set up an appointment to discuss this situation.

We often have team quizzes in class to review what we have been studying. _____ has a difficult time working with his team. He prefers to just shout out what he believes the answer to be. We have discussed that this is not fair to his team and are working on strategies to help him curb this impulse.

I would like to call you to discuss some trouble _____ has been having with self-control. He seems to be having difficulty keeping his hands to himself and often disrupts class by bothering his neighbors while they are trying to work.

Fairness

_____ has a wonderful understanding of fairness and is often sought out by other students to mediate disputes.

_____ has a terrific sense of fair play and demonstrates excellent sportsmanship.

Character Development

Fairness (continued)

_____ is really an excellent sportsman and sets a wonderful example for all of his class-mates. It is a joy to watch him play a game, regardless of whether he wins or loses.

_____ plays well with others and shows great maturity, even when she doesn't win.

_____ seems to really understand the importance of fairness. She takes turns and enjoys sharing with others.

I believe _____ needs help to develop better sportsmanship skills. He has a difficult time losing and a hard time being happy for his friends when they win. Perhaps you and I could get together and discuss ways to help him.

_____ has difficulty sitting still and waiting for her turn. She is working on this problem and trying hard to remember to let everyone have a turn in whatever we are doing.

_____ loves taking care of our class pets and does not want to do any other job. We have discussed the fact that it is only fair that everyone have a chance to feed our pets and that we must take turns with our class jobs.

_____ has real difficulty when it comes to taking turns in games. He does not have the patience to wait for his turn and often tries to take an extra turn. Hopefully this is just a stage that he will soon outgrow. If you experience this behavior at home, it may be helpful if you could talk about the importance of fair play.

I am noticing that _____ has been having trouble sharing materials with others. I have talked to her about this, and she has agreed to do better. I am looking forward to seeing progress in this area.

Citizenship

I am proud of _____. She takes her civic responsibilities very seriously and shows a desire to become more involved in community activities.

Citizenship (continued)

I am pleased to have _____ in my class. He consistently demonstrates a genuine understanding of other children's backgrounds. He is sensitive to cultural differences and really tries to build bridges of understanding between his classmates.

_____ is very open to learning about other cultures and beliefs. In fact, she really seems to enjoy learning about other cultures and lifestyles.

_____ is a delightful addition to our class. He respects others and follows the school rules. He sets a wonderful example of citizenship for the other students.

_____ does a great job keeping our classroom neat and orderly. She frequently volunteers to wash the boards and straighten the bookshelves at the end of the day. She seems quite proud to be a member of our class and encourages others to feel the same.

You should be very proud of _____. He is an excellent student and a responsible school citizen. He cares about his school and classroom and often volunteers for extra responsibilities in class.

Poor citizenship is becoming a problem for _____. She seems to have trouble following school rules and can be disrespectful to class property. I would like to arrange a conference to discuss ways for _____ to make better choices.

_____ does not seem to be interested in being a part of the classroom community. Perhaps it would help if you would also encourage him to do his classroom job each day and to help the other students tidy up the room at the end of the day.

Integrity

You can be very proud of _____. She tries to make good choices and will not compromise her integrity for others.

_____ consistently demonstrates strong, positive personal values and sets an excellent example for other students. It is a pleasure to have him in our class.

Integrity (continued)

You can be proud that _____ places such a high value on personal integrity. He is very concerned about what is right and expects the same from others. He is a wonderful role model for the whole class.

Although peer pressure can be a difficult thing to resist, _____ thinks for herself and tries to make the right decision regardless of what others decide.

_____ often demonstrates the kind of maturity and integrity everyone should have. For example, on the playground, he insists that everyone who wants to play in a game be allowed to play. He is supportive of all team members and understands that playing together as a team is more important than winning (or other example).

I am very proud of _____. She has really matured during this school year and has been a wonderful influence on the other students. We often break into small groups to do projects, and _____'s decisions in her group have always been guided by her strong values and high level of integrity.

It is wonderful to watch _____ with other students. Integrity is very important to him and he communicates this to his fellow students in all situations.

_____ seems to be easily influenced by others. It also appears she will compromise what is important to her in order to be accepted by the group. I would like to talk to you about the situation and see if you might have any insights.

_____ is a good student and sets high standards for himself. Recently, however, he has made some new friends, and I have seen some changes that may be of concern. It seems that when _____ is with his friends, their approval influences his decisions. I would like to discuss this situation with you and will call you next week.

_____ is very concerned about not fitting in, and this can affect her judgement at times. She knows what is right and only needs a little nudge to stay on course. I think we should talk about the situation and will call you next week.

_____ continues to reach for high personal and academic standards for himself and for those around him. He often seems disappointed, however, by others who fail to reach the high standards that he has set.

Perseverance

I applaud _____'s perseverance. She is always willing to try and gives her best effort in any situation, even when she does not meet with immediate success.

It is wonderful that _____ is always willing to try and give his best effort on any project. He often jumps in with both feet and his excitement is infectious. His enthusiasm and perseverance are appreciated by all.

_____ has shown great progress this quarter. She has really persevered through some tough challenges and her grades reflect her efforts. Her hard work has certainly paid off.

It appears _____ is easily defeated if not immediately successful. Hopefully some extra support in class will help. Perhaps you could offer extra encouragement at home when _____ brings home her next project. If you have any suggestions regarding this situation I would appreciate speaking with you.

_____ has little patience and tends to give up if something does not work on the first try. I have been working with him on this, but I think it is going to take some time and more effort on his part.

It is wonderful that _____ is always willing to try something new. Unfortunately, however, she is often willing to give up if it does not come easily. Perhaps we could talk and develop some strategies that might help.

Respect

_____ has come a long way this year. He is really much more respectful of the other students' feelings than he was at the beginning of the year. He has made many new friends and is really progressing nicely.

_____ is always respectful of the other students in the class.

_____ is respectful and polite to me and other adults in the school. He also shows respect for his classmates and their property.

Respect (continued)

_____ can often appear abrupt or disrespectful in a disagreement. He usually feels badly afterwards. He knows it is important to always show respect even when disagreeing. _____ and I have talked, and he has promised to work on it.

_____ is struggling when it comes to interacting with her classmates. When frustrated or upset, she appears to show little respect for the other children's feelings. I would like to talk to you about the situation and will call you to set up a conference.

_____ often shows little respect for other students' belongings. He will borrow something without asking and sometimes returns it damaged. This is causing problems with his classmates. We have discussed this on several occasions and are working on strategies that should help him.

_____ shows little respect for school rules that she feels are not important. We have discussed that the rules are for everyone and that she is expected to follow them. If there is not significant improvement soon I will call you so we can discuss the situation. It may be helpful if you could talk with her about the importance of school rules for everyone.

Peer Relations

Peer relations can be easy and wonderful for some children; they can be very difficult and challenging for others. The phrases below may help you better communicate to parents about a variety of issues that may arise in school regarding peer relationships.

Positive Peer Relations

_____ is very mature for his age and has made friends with many of the older students in school. I think this has been a very positive experience for him given his maturity level.

It is a joy to watch _____ in class. She has really come a long way. She has many friends and is able to take a leadership role in group activities.

_____ is always a willing volunteer and will help anyone in need. He is well liked by his classmates and is a delight to have in class.

I have really enjoyed having _____ in my class this year. She makes friends easily and is a good friend to every one of her classmates.

Needs Improvement

_____ is a popular, generally well-adjusted student. Recently, peer approval seems to have become very important to him. I will keep an eye on the situation and will call you if anything changes. Perhaps you could share any insights you might have with me.

_____ is doing fine academically, but she seems to be somewhat of a loner, only interacting with other students when forced. I just wanted you to be aware of the situation so we could both keep an eye on it.

I really enjoy having _____ in class. He always has an interesting view on whatever we are studying. Unfortunately, his uniqueness can make it difficult for him to fit in with the other students. Please feel free to call me any time to make an appointment to talk about this.

_____ makes friends easily and is very popular in class. Unfortunately she has a tendency to socialize when she should be working. I am working with her to improve in this area.

Needs Improvement (continued)

_____ is fairly immature for his age. Therefore he tends to make friends with younger students as he is more comfortable with them. He has been progressing nicely this year and by the beginning of the next school year should be making friends with students his own age.

_____ has been having a difficult time sharing ideas with her peers. She often appears to be afraid that her ideas will be challenged or that she might be wrong. I will continue to encourage her to participate and share her ideas in class.

_____ seems to be breaking away from his old friends and trying to befriend a new, much different group of students. I will monitor the situation and call you if I feel we need to talk.

_____ seems to feel uncomfortable with students who are different from her. We will be studying the cultures of all of the students in our class and talking about their similarities and differences. Hopefully, once _____ has an opportunity to gain a better understanding of other cultures and backgrounds, she will feel more comfortable with them.

_____ feels it is not "cool" to be smart. He often does not give his best effort, because he really wants to fit in. I will keep an eye on the situation and will call you if things do not change. Perhaps it would help if you encourage him to be his own person. If you feel we need to talk please call me at any time.

_____ seems to be having a difficult time in class making friends with the other students. I think we should talk. I will call you to set up a conference and see if you might have some suggestions.

It has been brought to my attention that lately _____ has become somewhat aggressive on the playground. I think we need to talk about this situation, and I will call you this week.

Recently _____ was in a situation where she tried to bite another student (or other action). This behavior concerns me, and I think we should talk about the situation as soon as possible.

Personal Development

Each child develops differently and in his own time. While some children mature quickly, others develop more slowly. It can be a pleasure watching them grow, as most strive to become the best they can be. There can also be bumps along the way that need to be addressed.

Peer Pressure

You should be very proud of _____. Although he takes other people's advice into consideration, he thinks for himself and makes good solid decisions. He should do well in school and life.

Although peer pressure can be difficult to resist, _____ really knows what he should be doing and does not let the group take him too far off track.

_____ appears not to care if he continues to do good work. Part of it may be that his peer group does not think it is "cool" to be smart. He is still doing very well, as he is a bright child who enjoys learning. I will closely monitor the situation to make sure he stays on track. I think we should talk. Any insights you have would be helpful.

When working independently, _____ has excellent instincts and does great work. In a group, however, she is easily influenced by others and will allow the group to go in a wrong direction rather than voicing a different opinion. I will try to help her become more comfortable in a group over the course of this year.

Effort

_____'s grades this quarter really reflect the effort she puts into her studies. She consistently strives to do her best.

_____ is a joy to have in class. He sets high standards for himself and works hard, putting forth a lot of effort to reach his goals.

_____'s work this quarter has been quite satisfactory. She is working on grade level, but she is quite bright and I believe she is capable of doing more. I would like to give her some independent work to push her to reach her potential.

Personal Development

Effort (continued)

_____ could be an excellent student but she does not seem motivated to work up to her potential. Hopefully being supportive and encouraging both at home and at school will help her excel.

_____ does all assignments and turns them in on time, but it is clear that he does not put forth his best effort unless it is something he loves. It is my hope that encouraging him to broaden his areas of interest may help.

_____ seems to not put forth a real effort on any assignment in which she is not interested. Unfortunately, social studies (or other area) is the only subject area she seems to like. I will continue to try and motivate _____ in school. Maybe you could help her broaden her interest with trips to a science or art museum. I am delighted that _____ loves social studies but would like to help her make a better effort in other subject areas.

Self-Esteem/Self-Confidence

_____ seems to really have the confidence to try new things. He is not afraid to take a risk.

_____ has a very healthy sense of self-worth. She is a sweet, well-adjusted child.

_____ needs some time to develop better leadership skills. To help with this, I will place him in some small group situations where he must take a leadership role.

_____ does not seem to be very happy with himself or his work. I would like to set up a meeting with you to discuss this and see if you might be able to share your impressions regarding this matter.

I am concerned because _____ seems to have lost a lot of weight over the last couple of months and still thinks she needs to lose more. You should be aware that she never eats her snack or lunch. I think it is important that we talk. Please call me to set up a meeting to discuss this situation.

It is of concern that _____ requires a lot of positive feedback and encouragement. He is a bright and popular student but seems to have a problem with self-esteem. I think we should set up a meeting to discuss this situation. I hope you may be able to offer some insights.

Maturity/Life Skills

It is a joy to have _____ in my class. She has been a wonderful influence on her classmates. Her curiosity and enthusiasm for learning are contagious. I hope she never loses them.

_____ is a happy and well-adjusted child who is quite mature for his age. He is also doing very well. He easily grasps complex concepts and exhibits a zest for learning.

_____ seems to be a little immature for his age and tends to seek attention when others are around. Maturity should take care of this situation, but in the meantime it is important for us not to encourage or reward this behavior.

When _____ is upset, she tends to cry and is then embarrassed. As she continues to mature and become comfortable with herself, these emotional swings should level out. I just wanted you to be aware that this seems to be a very difficult time for _____.

_____ is having a difficult time in class right now. All of his friends are a year to two younger as _____ is a little immature for his age. Hopefully time will take care of this issue but it is problematic for him right now. If you want to discuss this situation I will be available any afternoon this week.

Although _____ appears to be a little immature for his age in some areas, he is asking a lot of tough questions regarding sex, alcohol, and drugs. Please call me to discuss this issue.

Social/Communication Issues

_____ truly cares about other students and their feelings. If a child is left out of a game, she will play with him. If others appear unhappy, she will try to cheer them up. _____ really is a very special person. I am delighted to have her in my class.

It is a pleasure to have _____ in class. She gets along quite well with her classmates and cooperates well with others when working in a group situation.

_____ is a wonderful student. He is doing well academically and his conduct is impeccable. He seems to be very serious, though. I hope I can help him relax and enjoy our class more.

Personal Development

Social/Communication Issues (continued)

_____ is quite shy at school and seems to have only a few friends. She will work in a group, but only if assigned to one. Otherwise she prefers to work independently. She would rather be by herself on the playground than play with the other children. It might be helpful if you encouraged her to become involved in sports or some other outside activity that requires group involvement.

I am not sure exactly why, but _____ tends to come to class early and wants to stay late. It appears he wants more one-on-one time with an adult. I think we should set up a meeting to discuss this situation. I hope you may be able to offer some insights.

_____ has a need to tell me what other students have said or done. It creates problems for her with her classmates. This is a common concern with younger children. We have talked about the difference between telling and tattling. Reinforcing this at home might help.

_____ seems to have a hard time interacting with her classmates. She is quite bright and works well with everyone academically. Socially, however, she is a little immature. Hopefully time will take care of this issue, but it is difficult for her right now.

Personal Hygiene/Appearance

If you have an opportunity this week I would really appreciate it if we could talk. Our class has been working in small groups and the other members of _____'s group have been teasing her about her breath. It might be helpful if you check and make sure _____ brushes her teeth every morning. If she does, then you might want to talk with her dentist.

I have noticed that _____'s clothes are often rumpled and stained by the time he arrives at school. Maybe you could discuss this with _____, as perhaps there is something happening at the bus stop (or during his walk to school) to damage his clothing.

I would like to set up a time for us to meet. Personal hygiene is a very sensitive topic, but I feel we need talk about some of _____'s personal hygiene habits.

I know children can be sensitive about their appearance, but it seems that _____ does not take much pride in his appearance. I think it might be helpful if we could meet to discuss the situation.

Struggling Students

Not all students will be able to meet the expectations laid out by the curriculum. It is sometimes difficult to communicate this information effectively to parents, who often have a hard time believing their child could be struggling.

_____ is clearly giving his best effort, but he is having a very difficult time grasping the material he is expected to learn in _____ grade. I would like to discuss this situation with you.

_____ is a delightful student. She has many friends and excels in sports. Unfortunately, she is having a difficult time keeping up academically. I am concerned that _____ is really not ready for _____ grade. I would like to set up a conference with you.

As we have discussed, _____ is socially very immature. In addition, his academic skills are still not where they should be to go into the _____ grade. I would like to set up a conference with you to discuss his repeating this grade. I really think it would be best for him and key to his future success.

_____ has a difficult time settling down to work in class. She has a hard time understanding written directions and often needs to have them explained. Even when she understands the directions, she often cannot complete the task. I think it is important that we discuss the situation.

_____ is having a difficult time in school. He is having a hard time grasping many of the basic concepts and is therefore struggling academically. I believe it is important that we speak.

_____ always gives her best effort but struggles with almost every task. It also takes her much longer than the allotted time to finish an assignment. All of this pressure is taking a toll on _____, and I think it is important that we speak. I will call you to set up a time.

_____ has really given his best effort and made some real strides in math (or other subject). He is really struggling, however, with reading (or other subject). A summer program may help him get ready for _____ grade. I think you and I should discuss what may be best for _____.

_____ loves school and is a conscientious student but is struggling academically in all areas. I think it is important that we speak. I will call you to set up a time.

Average Students

Many students will achieve what is laid out in the curriculum. They will work hard, give their best effort and will always be right on grade level.

_____ is progressing nicely. She is working on grade level in all subject areas. She could use some help with the multiplication tables (or another skill). Perhaps if you spent a few minutes working on it together each night it would help.

_____ shows a good grasp of the basic _____ grade skills we have done so far. He is a hard worker and keeps trying until he understands the concept on which we are working.

_____ is making satisfactory progress in her studies this grading period. She is working right on grade level in all areas. She has an excellent attitude and always gives her best effort.

_____ is really progressing nicely in math (or other subject). The extra effort he has put into it is really paying off. He seems to have mastered his multiplication tables (or other skill) and is now ready to move on to division (or other skill).

_____'s reading comprehension has been showing steady improvement since she started doing extra work at home. She is right on grade level now and doing a good job in her reading group.

_____'s oral reading skills have improved dramatically this grading period. The extra reading you have been doing with him has really helped. He can now read any selection from his reader out loud in reading group. This has also helped improve his general self-confidence in class.

_____ is a delightful child. She takes pride in her work and is right on target, doing good solid _____ grade work.

_____ has a very positive attitude about school. He works hard and gets along well with his classmates. It is a pleasure to have him in class.

Gifted Students

Watching a child's mind grow and develop can be a wonderful experience. Students who are a quick study can offer challenges we might not have predicted. Sometimes we are able to offer them opportunities that might not otherwise be available.

_____ is a wonderful student and is truly excelling academically this year. He is doing so well you might want to consider enrolling him in our gifted program for next year.

_____ is truly a gifted math (or other subject) student. I have talked to the _____ grade teacher, and she is willing to let _____ move into one of her math classes. I would like to talk to you about this opportunity and will call you later this week.

_____ is an excellent student. He always seems to complete his work accurately and before anyone else. In order to help challenge _____, I will be getting him some higher-level material to work on when he finishes his other assignments.

_____ has an excellent attitude and is doing very well academically. She seems to be looking for a new challenge, and I would like to recommend her as a tutor for our peer-tutoring program if you have no objection. I think it could be a wonderful experience for _____.

You can be very proud of _____. She is doing very well academically and is well liked by her fellow students. _____ seems to particularly love science (or other subject) and really excels at it. You might want to see if there are any science programs in which you could enroll her for the summer. If you want to discuss this, please feel free to call me at any time.

_____ is an exceptional writer for his age. He has an extensive vocabulary and is an excellent speller. You might want to think about enrolling him in an outside writing class to encourage his talents. If you have any questions, please feel free to call me at any time.

It is really a pleasure to have _____ in class. She is an excellent role model and is doing very well academically. As we plan for next year we may want to consider having _____ take some of her classes with the _____ graders (next grade). She needs the extra challenge. I would like to discuss this with you and will call to set up a conference.

New Students/Transfer Students

Starting at a new school can be a very scary prospect for a student. There are new surroundings, new people, and new expectations.

_____ has been here only a short time so it is really too early to evaluate his academic performance. He has made a few friends and appears happy both in class and on the playground. He seems to be adjusting well to our class and school.

_____ seems to have made an excellent adjustment to her new school. She has made several friends, has joined in some team sports, and is doing fine academically. If things continue this way she should feel right at home soon.

It would be hard to make a fair evaluation of _____'s academic performance so far, as he has been here such a short time, but he appears to be making a great transition to a new school. He has already made a couple of friends, and the schoolwork he has done has been very good.

_____ is having some difficulty adjusting to her new class. She is especially quiet in class and never participates voluntarily. I will continue to encourage her to participate. Perhaps it would help if you also talk with her about the difficulties of transferring to a new school.

In class, it appears _____ has adjusted very well to being in a new school. There seem to be some problems on the playground, however. He really does not seem to play with anyone and often sits alone. Perhaps it would help if you could talk with him about this. I think it might also be helpful if we talked. Any insights you may have would be appreciated.

Since coming to our school _____ has made many new friends and seems to have a very active social life. I am a little concerned, however, with her academic performance. It is difficult to give an accurate evaluation, as she as not been here long, but I would like to talk with you.

_____ is still having a few problems adjusting to our class. It seems that his old school did not have homework every night during the week, and we do. He needs to understand that every assignment must be done and turned in the next day.

Testing Notification

Testing time can be a stressful time for everyone. Students are nervous, parents want their children to do well, and school administrators are concerned about how the test scores will reflect upon the school. It seems the teacher's job centers around keeping everyone on an even keel and making sure students are relaxed enough to do the best they can.

I wanted to notify you that in a few weeks we will be taking the _____ tests. _____ is well prepared, and I am sure he will perform to the best of his ability. At this point, helping _____ to relax and to not be nervous would be the best way to help him at home.

This year's standardized tests will be given in three weeks. There are a few hints I would like to give you to help ensure that _____ does her best. Please make sure she eats a good breakfast and is well rested before the tests. Reducing stress as much as possible is important. Sometimes doing something with your child that she particularly enjoys can help to relax her. If you have any questions regarding the upcoming tests, please call me.

This year we will be doing statewide testing of all _____ grade students. These tests are given in every public school in the state. They are used as one gauge to help evaluate how students are progressing. The best way for you to help _____ is to encourage him to relax and try to do his best.

This letter is to inform you that on _____ (day) of next week we will be doing standardized testing all day. In order for your child to do her best, it is important that she be well-rested, relaxed, and ready to take the tests. Please make sure she is on time, as testing will begin promptly at _____ A.M.

Results from the recent standardized tests are due to arrive on _____ (date). I would be happy to set up a conference to review the scores with you and address your questions and concerns. Please call me at your convenience.

Comments for the End of the Year

Can you believe it? Another year is just about over and summer break is almost here again. It is time to start planning how to help this class make the transition to a new grade and a new teacher. It is not always easy, but it can be exciting to review the year's accomplishments and the students' growth.

To Students

Congratulations! You made it! We had a great year and you were an important part of our class. You were a good student who worked hard and enthusiastically participated in learning. Your wonderful attitude served as a great role model for others to follow. Thank you for a great year.

We had a great year! Have a wonderful summer and enjoy the _____ grade. I know you will do well. I would encourage you to do as much reading over the summer as possible. Enclosed is a suggested reading list for next year. I think you will enjoy many of these books. I highlighted the ones I thought you would like best. Thank you for helping to make this an enjoyable and successful year. Enjoy your summer!

I really enjoyed having you in my class this year. You are a good student and have a great sense of humor (or other trait). I hope you have a terrific summer and lots of fun in _____ grade!

To Volunteers

The year is coming to a close and I wanted to take this opportunity to thank you. I appreciate all the help and support you gave the students and me this year. You have no idea how valuable your extra pair of hands has been. Your help allowed us to do projects that I otherwise would not have considered. I hope you and your family have a wonderful summer.

As this year comes to a close I wanted to take this opportunity to say thank you for all of your help this year. If you had not volunteered to bring goodies to our parties and pitch in on our class projects (or other jobs) we would not have had such a terrific year. Thank you again for all of your help and support. I will certainly miss you next year.

I want to take this opportunity to say thank you for all of your help this year. We could never have gone on all of the field trips we took without your volunteering to come with us. Our year was much richer and fuller thanks to all of your kindness.

To Volunteers (continued)

Thank you for being part of our class this year. The students and I appreciate everything you did for us and all the help you gave during this year. Many children can now read better or have improved math skills (or other skill) thanks to your time and patience. Thank you for all of your contributions. I look forward to seeing you in school next year.

To Parents

You should be very proud of _____. She worked very hard this year. She has made good progress and I am sure she will do well next year. She clearly enjoyed your class visits and handled it very well. It is not always easy to share your parent's attention. I wish you and your family a wonderful summer.

This year has gone by quickly, and I am sorry to see it end. This was an outstanding class and _____ was an important part of it. He has been an active participant all year and was always willing to help with any project. His upbeat, positive attitude added a bright spot to every day. I know he will do well next year in _____ grade.

I appreciate all of the hard work and effort _____ put into her school work this year. The thing I will remember most is her inquisitive nature (or other trait). I am delighted I had the opportunity to meet and get to know _____. I wish her the best in _____ grade.

We made it! The year has come to an end and although _____ faced some challenges, he was able to overcome them and have a very successful year. I hope he has a wonderful summer. He really earned it.

_____ worked very hard this year. I know she is looking forward to a great summer, and I hope she has time to play, daydream, relax, and read some good books. She deserves it after all of the hard work and effort she put in this year. I will really miss _____ next year; she was a great asset to our class.

Thank you for all of your cooperation and support with _____ this year. He has really grown and matured into a responsible student.

Summer/Break Suggestions

As summer approaches, or even interim breaks from year-round school, students are looking forward to play time. During a long summer break, students often lose much of what they were taught during the year. They may even forget some of the things they have learned during the shorter breaks of year-round school. Here are some things you may want to suggest that parents can do to encourage out of school learning.

- Encourage your child to read. If reading is a problem for him, encourage him to read newspaper articles or even comic books. (Most comic books are written on a fourth-grade reading level.)

- Get an assortment of workbooks that give practice in all of the basic skill areas. Encourage your child to do a couple of workbook pages a day.

- To help your child keep up in math, get a set of flash cards and drill for ten minutes every other day.

- Take a trip to a children's museum, an art museum, or a science museum.

- Let your child bake a cake from scratch. Let him follow the directions and measure out all of the ingredients.

- Spin a globe and pick a place to research. Help your child find ten interesting things about the place. For example, you might see what famous places exist there, how far away it is, what time it is there, and the language that is spoken there.

- Grow a vegetable garden. Have your child keep an observation book to record what is happening in the garden as it grows.

- Take a virtual trip with your child. Pick a place to visit. Plan how you are going to get there, how much it will cost, how much spending money you will need, what sites you are going to visit, and where you are going to stay. Do your research on the Internet and/or in the public library.

- Have your child write her own book.

- Challenge your child to invent a product and write a report on how he would bring it to market, including why the product should be brought to market and what its competition is.

- Help your child write a letter to a manufacturer of a product with which she was unhappy. Make sure she tells the manufacturer why she was disappointed and what she had expected.

- Encourage your child to keep a journal of his summer activities.

- Visit your state's web site on the Internet with your child and learn about its tourist attractions. Challenge your child to write an advertisement telling why someone should visit your state.

- Be a tourist for a day and visit historical places of interest in your area.

Positive Phrases

It is important in communication to use a positive approach whenever possible. The following are some general positive statements or phrases that may be of help to you.

has a good attitude

is very helpful in class

is always very cooperative

gets along well with others

is willing to help another student

is doing very well in _____

is really excelling in _____

is on time with assignments

is always willing to try

is a very hard-working student

never misses a homework assignment

takes pride in her work

is showing great improvement in _____

has a positive attitude

shows strong leadership qualities

is very conscientious

is very dependable

is always willing to participate in any class project

does well with oral presentations

has an excellent attendance record

has a great imagination

has made excellent progress in _____

always makes a great effort

is always eager to join in

communicates well orally

communicates well in writing

has excellent written communication skills

is always happy

sets a wonderful example for the entire class

is always courteous to others

is popular with his classmates

tries hard

is very talented in _____

acts maturely in any given situation

plays well with others

has a wonderful imagination

takes initiative

always gives her best effort

is very poised for a child his age

is very enthusiastic

has great interpersonal skills

is an exceptional student

is sensitive to other children's feelings

demonstrates excellent conduct

is always willing to share

follows directions well

always finishes assignments

is fun to have in class

is a pleasure to have in class

makes everyone smile

conceptualizes problems well

makes good decisions

is progressing well academically

excels at higher-level problem solving

Positive Phrases

is a delight to have in class

volunteers whenever help is needed

is always willing to volunteer

tries hard and is a high achiever

enjoys making others laugh

is a very capable student

seems to understand new concepts easily

always seem to enjoy _____

works well with others

responds well to suggestions

does excellent research

is always well prepared

is consistent in _____

is very mature

has matured a great deal

is kind to others

is eager to participate

makes friends easily

is very responsible

is very creative

always pays attention

has great listening skills

shows compassion for other students

always takes turns

keeps her work area neat

has wonderful people skills

manages his time well

tries on her own but knows when to ask for help

is always prepared for class

has excellent problem-solving skills

demonstrates higher-level thinking skills

works well in a group

works well independently

My Own Positive Phrases

(Add to your list by writing your favorite positive phrases below.)

Constructive Phrases

As you write report cards, notes home to parents, etc., it is often hard to find the right words for a given situation. The following is an assortment of thoughts, phrases, and comments designed to help you address a variety of situations during the year.

needs to be encouraged to _____

needs a lot of direction

needs specific direction

has a hard time following directions

is very shy

needs a lot of support

is inconsistent

daydreams

has a hard time focusing

has a difficult time staying on task

socializes too much

is having a hard time grasping _____

has a difficult time grasping new concepts

seems to need to tell me what other students have done

has leadership qualities

does not take an interest in her schoolwork

is not very popular with his classmates

has a hard time interacting with her classmates

seems to antagonize other students

has a hard time making friends

needs to work on developing self-control

has little self-control

needs constant encouragement

has trouble listening

does not follow the school rules

has a difficult time with classroom rules

is easily distracted

has a hard time working unsupervised

needs constant supervision

has a difficult time making the transition to another classroom or the lunchroom

does not adjust easily to change

often cries in class

occasionally/often falls asleep in class

has a hard time concentrating

does not make friends easily

is a very serious child

has a hard time expressing himself

could do better in school

has a hard time applying herself

needs to apply himself more

seems to be an underachiever

often gives away her lunch

seems to always pick at his lunch

has a hard time working with others

has trouble functioning in a small group

has a hard time staying on task when working in a small group

does not really seem to apply herself

likes to tell jokes all the time

has a hard time settling down to work

spends too much time socializing

enjoys making others laugh

may enjoy participating in a drama club

Constructive Phrases

disrupts class with jokes

can be quite disruptive

does not settle down and get to work on time

would benefit from more practice in _____

has trouble working independently

does not work well independently

can work independently for only short periods of time

has a lot of energy

would love it if we could spend the whole day on show and tell

needs to be constantly reminded about _____

has a hard time paying attention

wants to succeed in school

often tries to please everyone

is quite immature for his age

is much less mature than her classmates

needs to work on developing organizational skills

seems to have a hard time getting organized

has a hard time relating to others

calls other children names when angry

is easily influenced by others

has a strong personality

has a hard time deciding for himself

rushes through her work

always seems to be in a hurry

had a hard time remembering _____

often leaves his homework at home

needs to check her work before turning it in

works very slowly

cannot work within assigned time frames

has difficulty remembering more than one direction at a time

has trouble with higher-level problem solving

has trouble with critical thinking skills

does not use his time well

has difficulty planning her time

has a hard time estimating how long a task will take

does not use time to his advantage

is extremely sensitive and often misinterprets others' comments

can be very bossy

has poor impulse control

cannot keep busy once an assignment is done

often needs to think before she speaks

hurts other children's feelings by accident

is often aggressive

needs to respect other people's feelings

has a difficult time understanding another's point of view

needs to demonstrate more self-control

has a hard time talking in front of a group

loves going on field trips

does not take criticism well

is often not prepared

can be forgetful

would benefit from _____

76

Descriptive Words List

When you are writing report cards for an entire class, with each student having his own special gifts and talents, it is often hard to find the right words and enough words to describe each child accurately and differently. Below is a word bank to help support your efforts to succinctly, tactfully, or boldly write a unique report card for each student.

adjusts
admirable
adventuresome
affectionate
aggressive
ambitious
artistic
assertive
attentive
authoritative
bashful
beautiful
best
bossy
bright
capable
careless
caring
challenged
chatty
cheerful
compassionate
confident
concentration
conscientious
considerate
consistent
contributes
cooperative
courageous
courteous
creative
critical
daydreams
defiant
delightful
demanding
demonstrates

dependable
dependent
determined
difficult
disinterested
disobedient
disorganized
disruptive
domineering
dramatic
eager
effort
emotional
energetic
enthusiastic
excels
exceptional
expressive
extrovert
fair
flexible
focus
friendly
gifted
graceful
grasp
grown
happy
hard-working
hasty
helpful
hindering
hyperactive
imaginative
immature
impolite
improved
impulsive

inattentive
inconsistent
independent
influential
intelligent
interested
introvert
intuitive
inventive
involved
irresponsible
kind
leader
levelheaded
listens
manages
manipulative
mature
maturely
meaningful
messy
mischievous
neat
nervous
organized
original
outgoing
outstanding
participates
perceptive
personable
pleasant
poised
polite
popular
positive
problem-solver
proficient

Descriptive Words List

progressing
proud
quarrelsome
quiet
reliable
resentful
reserved
resilient
respectful
responds
responsible
restless
rigid
risk-taker
rude
sad
satisfactory
satisfied
self-confidence
self-directed
selfish

self-reliant
self-starter
sensitive
serious
shares
shy
skillful
sociable
social
strives
strong
stubborn
submissive
superb
sweet
talented
talkative
tattletale
temperamental
terrific
thorough

thoughtful
thoughtless
tired
troubled
truthful
understands
unfocused
unhappy
unreliable
unsociable
untruthful
verbal
vivacious
well-adjusted
well-behaved
well-liked
well-mannered
willful
willing
withdrawn
wonderful

My Own Descriptive Words

(Add to your list by writing your favorite descriptive words below.)

Parent Correspondence Log

Student's Full Name _____

Nickname (if any) _____ Date of Birth _____

Father's Name _____	Mother's Name _____
Address _____	Address _____
Phone (Daytime) _____	Phone (Daytime) _____
Phone (Evening) _____	Phone (Evening) _____
Phone (Cell) _____	Phone (Cell) _____
E-mail _____	E-mail _____
Fax _____	Fax _____

Date	Form of Communication	Comments	Follow-up

Carson-Dellosa CD-2703

A Note from the Teacher

Date: _____

_____

_____

_____

_____

Teacher Signature: _____

☐ Parent Signature: _____
(Please sign and return if box is checked.)

© Carson-Dellosa CD-270

A Note from the Teacher

Date: _____

_____

_____

_____

_____

Teacher Signature: _____

☐ Parent Signature: _____
(Please sign and return if box is checked.)

© Carson-Dellosa CD-2703

© Carson-Dellosa CD-270